POLICE OFFICER INTERVIEW
QUESTIONS AND ANSWERS
(New core competencies)

by Richard McMunn

Orders: Please contact How2become Ltd, Suite 3, 50 Churchill Square Business Centre, Kings Hill, Kent ME19 4YU.

Orders via Gardners.com or through How2become.com by contacting the email address info@how2become.co.uk.

ISBN 978-1-910202-13-5

First published 2014

Typeset for How2become Ltd by Anton Pshinka.

Printed in Great Britain for How2become Ltd by Bell & Bain Ltd, 303 Burnfield Road, Thornliebank, Glasgow G46 7UQ.

PREFACE BY AUTHOR RICHARD MCMUNN

Over the past few years I have coached and helped literally hundreds of people to prepare for different selection processes and interviews, including police officers. I spent 17 years in Kent Fire and Rescue Service, during which time I worked at the Fire Service Training Centre. During my stint at the Training Centre I was involved in:

- Leading and managing firefighter trainee courses (4 in total)
- Marking application forms for new applicants
- Sitting on interview panels assessing potential trainee firefighters to join the job

I have no doubt that all of this experience has helped me to become successful as an author, coach and mentor. I have a genuine passion for helping people like you to achieve their goals. However, none of this is possible without the co-operation of the student; in this case, you. It is crucial that you spend plenty of time on your police officer interview preparation. You must leave no stone unturned and prepare your responses to every question in this book. Follow my advice carefully and I guarantee you will be fully prepared and confident when you walk through the interview room door, on the actual day of your interview.

I joined the Fire Service on January the 25th 1993 after completing four years in the Fleet Air Arm branch of the Royal Navy. In the build up to joining the Fire Service I embarked on a comprehensive training programme that would see me pass the selection process with relative ease. The reason why I passed the selection process with ease was solely due to the preparation and hard work that I had put in during the build-up.

I have always been a great believer in preparation. Preparation was my key to success, and it is also yours. Without the right level of preparation you will be setting out on the route to failure. The police force is very hard to join, but if you follow the steps that I have compiled within this guide then you will increase your chances of success dramatically. Remember, you are learning how to be a successful candidate, not a successful police officer.

The police force has changed a great deal over the past few years, and even more so in how it assesses potential candidates for police constable positions. The UK Police Force needs people who represent the community in which it serves. It needs people from different backgrounds, different cultures, different ages, different sexual orientations and different genders. Basically, the community in which we live in, is diverse in nature and therefore, so should the police force be if it is to achieve its aim of providing a high level of service the public deserves.

As you progress through this guide you will notice that the qualities (core competencies) required to be a competent police officer are a common theme. You must learn these competencies and also be able to demonstrate them at interview, if you are to have any chance of successfully passing the selection process.

I wish you all the very best in your pursuit to passing the police officer interview. Now, let's get started!

Best wishes

Richard McMunn

P.S. We are now running a series of 1-day training courses to help people like you prepare for the police officer selection process. The course is run by former serving police officers and is GUARANTEED to put you ahead of the competition.

Visit the website below to find out more:

www.PoliceCourse.co.uk

ABOUT THE POLICE OFFICER ASSESSMENT CENTRE INTERVIEW

ABOUT THE POLICE OFFICER ASSESSMENT CENTRE INTERVIEW

During this section of the guide I want to answer some of the more common questions people ask me. The answers will help you to hone your preparation in the right areas.

If you have reached this stage of the selection process then the police force you have applied to join are interested in employing you and they want to meet you face-to-face in order to see what you are like as a person, and also whether you really do have the skills required to become a competent officer.

Before I provide my sample interview questions and tips, let me answer a question that I get asked time and time again by police officer applicants: *"What's the best way to prepare for the interview, Richard?"*

Here's my response:

"The police officer assessment centre interview is used as a means to assess your potential to become a competent officer. Fitness is important to the role but it is not the 'be all and end all'. Yes, you must demonstrate a good level of fitness, but there are more important elements to demonstrate, in my opinion.

*The interviewer will be looking for 'evidence' of where you can match the assessable core competencies. The word **evidence** is pivotal and I suggest you have it at the forefront of your mind during your preparation. You have to provide as much evidence as possible as to how you match the assessable core competencies. The reason for this is simple: if you can provide evidence then there is a far greater chance of you succeeding as a police officer on the frontline. Let's face it, anyone can say that they are a 'good team-worker', or 'good at working with people from different backgrounds'; however, providing evidence that backs up those statements is an entirely different thing altogether. So, during your preparation you should concentrate on providing specific examples of where you can meet the competencies being assessed, more on this later.*

You should also think very carefully about why you want to become a police officer. It's all well and good say that you've wanted to do this since you were a little boy or girl, but responses like this will gain few marks. You have to have a genuine reason for wanting to join; something like 'wanting to make a difference to your community' is a much better reason than 'wanting to catch criminals'.

Finally, and this is just a big a factor than any other, your 'likability' will be key to your success. Yes, there are rules and guidelines that the interviewer must adhere to when interviewing potential candidates, but you can never take away the personal element. You should try hard to come across as a genuine, reliable, professional and conscientious individual. Do not be arrogant or over-confident at the either the assessment centre interview or the final interview, and always try to demonstrate your willingness to learn and be part of the wider police team."

If I were preparing for the police officer interview today, I would first of all ask myself the following three questions:

Q1. What areas will they assess me on during the interview?

Q2. What would they expect to see from successful interview candidates?

Q3. Can I provide 'evidence' of where I meet the assessable competencies?

I will then write down my perceived answers to these questions and I get the following responses:

A1. They will ask me questions that are based around the four assessable core competencies. They will also assess how I communicate orally and how I structure my responses to the questions being asked. They will require me to provide 'specific' examples of where I already have experience in each of the competency-based areas.

A2. They would expect successful candidates to provide specific examples that relate to the competency-based questions. They would also expect my responses to the interview questions to be concise, relevant, well structured and in a logical sequence.

A3. I would need to think seriously about the type of evidence I have to demonstrate that I would make a good police officer. For example, one of the assessable qualities required to become a police officer is that of **working with others**; or in other words, teamwork. I would need to be able to provide a number of specific examples of where I have worked as part of a team and demonstrated my competence in this area. I would also need to write down specific examples of where I can match the other assessable competency areas. This will mean getting a copy of the new core competencies being assessed that are relative to the role and working through them carefully, thinking of examples of where I match each and every one of them.

Now that I have my answers to the above questions, I will set out another simple plan that dictates exactly what I am going to do (action points), to put those answers right. In this particular case it will look something like this:

ACTION POINT 1 - I will learn the core competencies thoroughly and I will think of specific examples where can match each and every one of them. I will use the STAR method when constructing my responses to the interview questions, which will allow me to put them across in a concise and logical manner.

ACTION POINT 2 - I will visit my local police station and speak to the officer's and PCSO's about their role so that I can find out more about what it is like to be a front-line police officer. I will also visit the website of the police force I am applying to join and learn about the proactive side to the job in addition to the reactive side.

Your preparation should start weeks before your interview date, not the night before!

Frequently asked questions

The interview is designed to assess whether or not you have the qualities, skills and experience to carry out the role of a police officer. In particular, the interview will seek to assess whether or not you can meet the core competencies that are relevant to the role. You will be assessed directly against 4 core competencies, these being Professionalism, Public Service, Working with Others and Service Delivery. You will be asked just one question from each competency and you will have up to 5 minutes to provide your response. Once the interviewer has asked you the question, he or she will then hand you a written copy of the question for you to refer to. The interviewer may then ask you probing questions in order extract the required information from you. In addition to the four competencies, you will also be assessed indirectly with regards to how you communicate, so make sure your responses are concise, structured and logical.

TIP - Read and understand the core competencies before you attend the interview and be ready to provide specific examples of where your skills and experience meet each one.

How long will the interview last for?

The interview will last no longer than 20 minutes. My advice is to respond to the questions sufficiently to provide enough quality evidence. Don't waffle, but instead provide good, solid responses. You should practice a mock interview before you attend the assessment centre so that you get to try out you responses before the actual day.

What should I wear to the interview?

You will not normally be assessed on your dress but I strongly advise that you wear a formal outfit such as a suit. Make sure your shoes are clean and polished and do not wear white socks or ties with cartoon characters on them! Remember that you are applying to join a disciplined service. If you cannot dress smart then how will you be able to wear your uniform with pride? Police officer's are role models for the service they work for. You should have good personal hygiene and be capable of wearing your uniform in a smart and presentable manner.

Is everyone asked the same set of questions?

Yes they are. This is so that the process is fair and everyone gets the same chance. Therefore, you should refrain from telling anyone the questions you were asked at the interview, as they could be your direct competition.

How many people will be on the panel?

There will usually be just one person conducting the interview. He or she will either be a serving police officer or someone whom the police force has chosen from the community. On the odd occasion, there may also be another assessor in the room who will be making sure the interview is run in accordance with the police force's policies and procedures.

How will the interview commence?

The interviewer will ask you to sit down and they will introduce themselves to you. There will be a glass of water on the table in front of you and you will be asked to make yourself comfortable. Whilst it is ok to make yourself feel comfortable, do remember that you are being assessed so make sure you keep an eye on your interview technique.

The interviewer will then explain the purpose of the interview to you. They will state that they are going to ask you for specific examples of what you have done in different situations. It is okay to draw from examples from home, work, education or hobbies. It is advisable that you draw from a variety of different experiences.

The most important piece of advice I can give you

Throughout this guide so far I have made reference to the assessable core competencies. If I were preparing for the interview right now I would take each competency individually and prepare a detailed response setting out where I meet the requirements of it. Your response to each question that relates to the competencies must be 'specific' in nature. This means that you must provide an example of where you have already demonstrated the skills that are required under each one. Do not fall into the trap of providing a 'generic' response that details what you 'would do' if the situation arose.

Try to structure your responses in a logical and concise manner. The way to achieve this is to use the 'STAR' method of interview question response construction:

Situation

Start off your response to the interview question by explaining what the 'situation' was and who was involved.

Task

Once you have detailed the situation, explain what the 'task' was, or what needed to be done.

Action

Now explain what 'action' you took, and what action others took. Also explain why you took this particular course of action.

Result

Explain what the outcome or result was following your actions and those of others. Try to demonstrate in your response that the result was positive because of the action you took.

Finally, consider explaining to the interviewer what you would do differently if the same situation arose again, if you feel there was room for improvement. It is good to be reflective at the end of your responses. This demonstrates a level of maturity and it will also show the interviewer that you are willing to learn from every experience.

Now let's take a look at each of the four core competencies individually (in no particular order), before we move onto my sample assessment centre interview questions and answers.

WORKING WITH OTHERS

Works co-operatively with others to get things done, willingly giving help and support to colleagues. Is approachable, developing positive working relationships? Explains things well, focusing on the key points and talking to people using language they understand. Listens carefully and asks questions to clarify understanding, expressing own views positively and constructively. Persuades people by stressing the benefits of a particular approach, keeps them informed of progress and manages their expectations. Is courteous, polite and considerate, showing empathy and compassion. Deals with people as individuals and addresses their specific needs and concerns. Treats people with respect and dignity, dealing with them fairly and without prejudice regardless of their background or circumstances.

Once you become a police officer you will need to be effective at working with others, and I don't just mean working with other police officers. You will have to communicate and work with other stakeholders and organisations, too, such as the Fire Service, the Local Authority and the Ambulance Service. During the interview you will need to demonstrate that you already have the ability to work as part of a team and that you are also capable of working other people, regardless of their age, gender, background, religious beliefs, sexual orientation or otherwise.

PUBLIC SERVICE

Demonstrates a real belief in public service, focusing on what matters to the public and will best serve their interests. Understands the expectations, changing needs and concerns of different communities, and strives to address them. Builds public confidence by talking with people in local communities to explore their viewpoints and break down barriers between them and the police. Understands the impact and benefits of policing for different communities, and identifies the best way to deliver services to them. Works in partnership with other agencies to deliver the best possible overall service to the public.

This competency is all about serving the public. Police officer's have to provide an excellent level of service and this means having an understanding of the 'needs' of both individuals within their community as well as the many diverse groups that make up society. When preparing for this competency I recommend you try to think of specific examples when you have delivered excellent customer service either on your own or as part of a group. The interviewer may also look for evidence of how you adapted to the changing needs of an individual or group of people.

SERVICE DELIVERY

Understands the organisation's objectives and priorities, and how own work fits into these. Plans and organises tasks effectively, taking a structured and methodical approach to achieving outcomes. Manages multiple tasks effectively by thinking things through in advance, prioritising and managing time well. Focuses on the outcomes to be achieved, working quickly and accurately and seeking guidance when appropriate.

Police officers need to be organised and be capable of working in a methodical manner, if they are to meet the high expectations of the public they serve. During the interview you may be required to provide a response which details of a specific situation where you carried out a difficult task. During your response you will need to provide details of how you planned the task, prioritised action points and also managed your time effectively in order to meet the outcomes/expectations.

PROFESSIONALISM

Acts with integrity, in line with the values and ethical standards of the Police Service. Takes ownership for resolving problems, demonstrating courage and resilience in dealing with difficult and potentially volatile situations. Acts on own initiative to address issues, showing a strong work ethic and demonstrating extra effort when required. Upholds professional standards, acting honestly and ethically, and challenges unprofessional conduct or discriminatory behaviour. Asks for and acts on feedback, learning from experience and developing own professional skills and knowledge. Remains calm and professional under pressure, defusing conflict and being prepared to step forward and take control when required.

Police officers are required to act with a high degree or professionalism and integrity at all times. They must follow policies, rules and procedures and be capable of upholding the principles and ethics of the police force. As such, they need to have the confidence to challenge inappropriate behaviour and also demonstrate resilience when required, stepping in to take control of deteriorating situations with a view to resolving them.

Now that we have briefly covered each of the four assessable core competencies, let's move on to the all-important sample questions and answers. Please note: the questions in the next section of the guide are not guaranteed to be the exact ones you will get asked at the interview. They are provided for guidance and training purposes only.

SAMPLE INTERVIEW QUESTIONS AND RESPONSES
(Assessment centre interview)

SAMPLE INTERVIEW QUESTIONS AND RESPONSES

Within this section of the guide I will provide you with a number of sample interview questions that are specifically for the assessment centre interview. Wherever possible, I will also provide brief details on what I believe makes a strong response, and what I believe makes a weak one.

Whilst you will not be asked every question that follows, they will all give you a great hand during your preparation and I strongly recommend you prepare a response for each and every one of them. In order to assist you in your preparation I have provided a blank space following many of the questions for you to write down your own sample response, based on the information I have provided. Please note: the examples that you provide during the interview must be real. Do not make up situations and also do not copy the ones I have provided within the guide.

Plenty of hard work and determination is needed here, so be prepared to knuckle down and put in the effort.

INTERVIEW QUESTIONS AND ANWERS BASED ON THE FOUR ASSESSABLE CORE COMPETENCIES

The first competency that we will look at deals with Working with Others and this will demonstrate the extent to which you work effectively with other people, either at work, in the community or otherwise.

Let's quickly remind ourselves of this competency:

Works co-operatively with others to get things done, willingly giving help and support to colleagues. Is approachable, developing positive working relationships. Explains things well, focusing on the key points and talking to people using language they understand. Listens carefully and asks questions to clarify understanding, expressing own views positively and constructively. Persuades people by stressing the benefits of a particular approach, keeps them informed of progress and manages their expectations. Is courteous, polite and considerate, showing empathy and compassion. Deals with people as individuals and addresses their specific needs and concerns. Treats people with respect and dignity, dealing with them fairly and without prejudice regardless of their background or circumstances.

Q1 – Tell me about a time when you have contributed to the effective working of a team?

How to structure your response:

- What was the size and purpose of the team?

- Who else was in the team?

- What was YOUR role in the team? (Explain your exact role)

- What did you personally do to help make the team effective?

- What was the result?

Strong response

To make your response strong you need to provide specific details of where you have worked with others effectively, and more importantly where YOU have contributed to the team. Try to think of an example where there was a problem within a team and where you volunteered to make the team work more efficiently. It is better to say that you identified there was problem within the team rather than that you were asked to do something by your manager or supervisor.

Make your response concise and logical so that you score high with regards to 'communication'.

Weak response

Those candidates who fail to provide a specific example will provide weak answers. Do not fall into the trap of saying 'what you would do' if this type of situation arose.

Sample response

"I like to keep fit and healthy and as part of this aim I play football for a local Sunday team. We had worked very hard to get to the cup final and we were faced with playing a very good opposition team who had recently won the league title. The team consisted of 11 players who regularly spend time together during training sessions and at social events. After only ten minutes of play, one of our players was sent off and we conceded a penalty as a result. Being one goal down and 80 minutes left to play we were faced with a mountain to climb. However, we all remembered our training and worked very hard in order to prevent any more goals being scored. Due to playing with ten players, I had to switch positions and play as a defender,

something that I am not used to. Apart from being a defender I felt my role was to encourage the other players to keep going and to not give up until the final whistle had sounded. All the other players supported each other tremendously and the support of the crowd really pushed us on. The team worked brilliantly to hold off any further opposing goals and after 60 minutes we managed to get an equaliser. The game went to penalties in the end and we managed to win the cup. I believe I am an excellent team player and can always be relied upon to work as an effective team member at all times. I understand that being an effective team member is very important if the police force is to provide a high level of service to the community in which it serves. Effective teamwork is also essential in order to maintain the high safety standards that are set by the police."

Now take the time to use the blank space on the following page to prepare your own response to this question.

YOUR RESPONSE TO THIS QUESTION

Q1 – Tell me about a time when you have contributed to the effective working of a team?

Q2 – Tell me about a time when you helped someone who was distressed or in need of support.

How to structure your response:

- What was the situation?
- Why did you provide the help? (Whether you were approached or you volunteered – TIP: It is better to say you volunteered!)
- What did you do to support the individual?
- What specifically did you do or say?
- What was the result?

Strong response

Again, make sure you provide a specific example of where you have helped someone who was in distress or who needed your support. Try to provide an example where the outcome was a positive one as a result of your actions. If the situation was one that involved potentially dangerous surroundings (such as a car accident), did you consider the safety aspect and did you carry out a risk assessment of the scene?

Weak response

Candidates who provide a weak response will be generic in their answering. The outcome of the situation will generally not be a positive one.

Sample response

"One evening I was sat at home watching television when I heard my next door neighbours smoke alarm sounding. This is not an unusual occurrence as she is always setting off the alarm whilst cooking. However, on this occasion, something was different as the alarm did not normally sound so late at night. I got up out of my chair and went to see if she was OK. She is a vulnerable, elderly lady and I always look out for her whenever possible.

When I arrived next door I peered through the window and noticed my neighbour sat asleep on the chair in the front room. Wisps of smoke were coming from kitchen so I knew that she was in trouble. I immediately ran back into my house and dialled 999 calmly. I asked for the Fire Service and the Ambulance Service and explained that a person was stuck inside the house with a fire burning in the kitchen. I provided the call operator as much information as possible including landmarks close to our road to make it easier for the Fire Service to find. As soon as I got off the phone I immediately went round the back of my house to climb over the fence. Mrs Watson, my neighbour, usually leaves her back door unlocked until she goes to bed. I climbed over the fence and tried the door handle. Thankfully the door opened. I entered into the kitchen and turned off the gas heat which was burning dried up soup. I then ran to the front room, woke up Mrs Watson and carried her carefully through the front door, as this was the nearest exit.

I then sat Mrs Watson down on the pavement outside and placed my coat around her. It wasn't long before the Fire Service arrived and they took over from there on in. I gave them all of the details relating to the incident and informed them of my actions whist in the kitchen."

Now take the time to use the blank space on the following page to prepare your own response to this question.

YOUR RESPONSE TO THIS QUESTION

Q2 – Tell me about a time when you helped someone who was distressed or in need of support.

Q3 – Can you give an example of when you have worked closely with an individual or group of people from a different background to yourself?

How to structure your response:

- What was the situation?
- Why was the task you and the other individual or group had to achieve?
- What did you do to work more effectively with the other person or group?
- What did you do to make sure the task ran smoothly?
- What was the end result?

Strong response

Make sure you provide a specific example of where you have worked with an individual or group of people who were from a different background to yourself. Try to provide an example where the outcome was a positive one as a result of yours and their actions. If you encountered any difficulties during the activity, tell the interviewer what you did to overcome these.

Weak response

Candidates who provide a weak response will be generic in their answering. The outcome of the situation will generally not be a positive one and they will not structure their response in a logical and concise manner.

Sample response

"Whilst working for a construction company we received news that a new group of workers were coming from Poland to spend 6-months on a project that I was heavily involved in. As soon as I heard the news I went to see my line manager to inform him that I would like to help the group settle in to their new surroundings and also help them understand the requirements of the project. After a short meeting with my manager, he agreed that I could take up this voluntary role.

Before the workers arrived, I sat down and put together an action plan of what I wanted to achieve and how I would do it. The action plan included how I would help the new workers to settle in by showing them around the construction company, introducing them to key members of staff and also providing them with a point of contact if at all they ever needed any support during their 6-month stay. I felt it was important to create an action plan, as I wanted things to be organised, methodical and to also meet my objectives.

As soon as the workers arrived I made contact with the groups leader and informed him that I would be their main point of contact during their stay with our company. I started to get as much information about the group, speaking to them on first name terms in order to break down any barriers that might be present. As soon as I had established a rapport with the group I then sat down with them to discuss the project. I communicated with them in a pace that they could understand and established each group members' strengths and weaknesses. Once I had gathered all of the facts we then commenced an initial 2-week familiarisation period that enabled each group member to learn their role within the project and also understand the teams objectives. Throughout this period I supported the group and worked closely with them to achieve the project goals. Once the familiarisation period was complete, we then commenced work on the project. Everyone within the group was clear with regards to the end goal and also, more importantly, the timeframe in which it had to be completed.

The end result was extremely positive. Not only did we work effectively as a team but we also managed to complete the end goal four weeks ahead of schedule. My manager was so impressed with the work I undertook with the group that he appointed me as company liaison manager for all future overseas visitors who came to the organisation."

Now take the time to use the blank space on the following page to prepare your own response to this question.

YOUR RESPONSE TO THIS QUESTION

Q3 – Can you give an example of when you have worked closely with an individual or group of people from a different background to yourself?

Q4 – Describe a time when you have helped to support diversity in a team, school, college or organisation.

How to structure your response:

- What was the situation?

- What prompted the situation?

- What were the diversity issues?

- What steps did you take to support others from diverse backgrounds?

- What specifically did you say or do?

- What was the result?

Strong response

This type of question is difficult to respond to, especially if you have little or no experience in this area. However, strong performing candidates will be able to provide clear details and examples of where they have supported diversity in a given situation. Their response will be specific in nature and it will clearly indicate to the panel that they are serious about this important subject.

Weak response

Weak responses are generic in nature and they fail to answer the question that is being asked. Many candidates are unable to provide a specific response to this type of question.

Sample response

"Whilst working in an office I noticed that a new member had joined our team. The lady was confined to a wheelchair and for some strange reason my boss decided to put her in an office which was a fair distance from the exit, toilet and kitchen facilities. I immediately picked up on this and decided that something needed to be done in order to help make her life a bit easier. Although the office shape and design met current legal requirements for access, I felt it was unfeasible to expect the new member of the team to have such a struggle to get access to these everyday facilities.

I started off by approaching my boss and asking him if I could make a suggestion. I started to put my case over to him and explained that I would be more than happy to offer the lady my office, as it was much closer to the facilities. My boss agreed that it was a good idea and he felt rather guilty that he had not even considered the issue in the first place.

I then went over to my new colleague and introduced myself. I quietly asked her if she would like to swap offices with me and explained that the facilities would be a lot closer for her if she took up my offer. I also apologised for her being put so far away from them in the first place. She thanked me for my consideration and took me up on my offer. I then assembled a small team of workers who assisted me in moving desks and computers. The lady soon settled into her new office where she had much better access to the exit and the facilities.

Finally, I suggested to my boss that we should all attend a company diversity awareness course to raise awareness of these important issues. He agreed and we all attended the course over a period of four weeks."

Now take the time to use the blank space on the following page to prepare your own response to this question.

YOUR RESPONSE TO THIS QUESTION

Q4 – Describe a time when you have helped to support diversity in a team, school, college or organisation.

The next competency we will look at deals with **Professionalism**. Let's quickly remind ourselves what this competency covers:

Acts with integrity, in line with the values and ethical standards of the Police Service. Takes ownership for resolving problems, demonstrating courage and resilience in dealing with difficult and potentially volatile situations. Acts on own initiative to address issues, showing a strong work ethic and demonstrating extra effort when required. Upholds professional standards, acting honestly and ethically, and challenges unprofessional conduct or discriminatory behaviour. Asks for and acts on feedback, learning from experience and developing own professional skills and knowledge. Remains calm and professional under pressure, defusing conflict and being prepared to step forward and take control when required.

Q5 – Tell me about a time when acted on your own initiative to solve a problem?

How to structure your response:

- What was the problem and how did you approach the task?

- Were there any rules or instructions that you had to follow?

- What did you do to complete the work as directed?

- What was the result?

- How did you feel about completing the task in this way?

Strong response

Police officers must be able to act on their own initiative, especially during potentially difficult and volatile situations. Try to think of a situation, either at work or otherwise, where you have achieved this in a calm, resilient and controlled manner. Make your response specific in nature. If you had to follow specific instructions, rules or procedures then this is a good thing to tell the interviewer.

Weak response

Weak responses are generic in nature and usually focus on a candidate's own views on how a problem should be resolved, rather than providing a specific situation. The candidate may also demonstrate anger or a tendency to 'fight fire with fire' when dealing with this type of difficult situation.

Sample response

"I am currently working as a sales assistant for a well-known retailer. More recently I achieved a temporary promotion and was required to manage the shop one busy Saturday afternoon.

At approximately 2pm a customer entered the shop and approached the desk. He began complaining to a member of staff (Julie) about a coat he had purchased from our company the week before. As Julie listened to his complaint he started to get quite irate and began to raise his voice. I could see Julie becoming upset. The gentlemen then started to be verbally abusive her and at that point I calmly intervened. I introduced myself as the store manager and informed the gentleman that I would be dealing with his complaint from here on in. I then went on to tell him that I would do all I could to resolve his complaint, but that I would not tolerate any form of aggressive, confrontational or abusive language. I also warned him that any further use of such communication would be reported to the police, inline with company policy. This immediately had the effect of calming down the customer as he realised that he had already crossed the line with his comments to the other member of staff. He immediately apologised to Julie.

I then asked the customer to explain exactly what had happened and reassured him that I would resolve the issue. Whilst he explained his complaint I maintained an open and relaxed body position in order to diffuse any potential conflict and utilised effective listening skills. After listening carefully to his compliant I then explained how I would resolve it for him. In line with company policy the customer received a replacement coat in addition to a full refund, to which he was very happy with. I feel that throughout the situation, I maintained a resilient and professional stance, yet still managed to resolve the customers complaint to their satisfaction."

Now take the time to use the blank space on the following page to prepare your own response to this question.

YOUR RESPONSE TO THIS QUESTION

Q5 – Tell me about a time when acted on your own initiative to solve a problem?

Q6 – Tell me about a time when you sought to improve the way that you do things following feedback from someone else?

How to structure your answer:

- What was the improvement that you made?

- What prompted this change?

- What did you personally do to ensure that the change was successful?

- What was the result?

Strong response

Part of the police officer's role is to respond to feedback and act on your own initiative in order to improve. Stronger performing candidates are able to provide a response that demonstrates a voluntary willingness to improve or change the way they do things.

Weak response

Candidates who are unable to identify where improvements are needed will generally provide weak responses. Once again the response will be generic in nature and lack any substance or specific evidence.

Sample response

"I currently work as a telecommunications engineer and I have been doing this job for nine years now. I am very well qualified and can carry out the tasks that form part of my job description both professionally and competently. However, with the introduction of wireless telecommunications I started to feel a little bit out of my depth. Wireless telecommunications basically provides telephone, Internet, data, and other services to customers through the transmission of signals over networks of radio towers. The signals are transmitted through an antenna directly to customers, who use devices, such as mobile phones and mobile computers, to receive, interpret, and send information. I knew very little about this section of the industry and decided to ask my line manager for an appraisal. During the appraisal I raised my concerns about my lack of knowledge in this area and she agreed to my request for continuing professional training in this important area.

I was soon booked on a training course which was modular in nature and took seven weeks to complete. During the training I personally ensured that I studied hard, followed the curriculum and checked with the course tutor periodically to assess my performance and act on any feedback they offered. At the end of the training I received a distinction for my efforts.

I now felt more comfortable in my role at work and I also started to apply for different positions within the company that involved wireless technology. For the last 6 months I have been working in the wireless telecommunications research department for my company and have excelled in this new area of expertise."

Now take the time to use the blank space on the following page to prepare your own response to this question.

YOUR RESPONSE TO THIS QUESTION

Q6 – Tell me about a time when you sought to improve the way that you do things following feedback from someone else?

Q7 – Tell me about a time when you have taken it upon yourself to learn a new skill or develop an existing one?

How to structure your response:

- What skill did you learn or develop?

- What prompted this development?

- When did this learning or development occur or take place?

- How did you go about learning or developing this skill?

- What was the result?

- How has this skill helped you since then?

Strong response

Police officers are required to learn new skills, policies and procedures throughout the duration of their career. They will attend on-going training courses and they will also read up on new procedures and policies. In order to maintain a high level of professionalism, they must be committed to continuous development. Try to think of an occasion when you have learnt a new skill, or where you have taken it upon yourself to develop your knowledge or experience in a particular subject. Follow the above structured format to create a strong response.

Weak response

Those candidates who have not taken on any new development or learning will be unable to provide a strong response. They will provide a response where they were told to learn a new skill, rather than taking it upon themselves. There will be no structure to their learning or development and they will display a lack of motivation whilst learning.

Sample response

"Although I am in my late thirties I had always wanted to learn to play the guitar. It is something that I have wanted to do for many years, but have never had the time to learn, until recently. One day I was watching a band play with my wife at my local pub and decided there and then that I would make it my mission to learn to play competently. The following day I went onto the Internet and searched for a good guitar tutor in my local area. Luckily, I managed to find one within my town who had a very good reputation for teaching. I immediately booked a block of lessons and started

my first one within a week. My development in the use of playing the guitar progressed rapidly and I soon achieved grade 1 standard. Every night of the week I would dedicate at least 30 minutes of time to my learning, in addition to my one hour weekly lesson. I soon found that I was progressing through the grades quickly, which was due to my level of learning commitment and a desire to become competent in playing the instrument.

I recently achieved level 4 and I am now working to level 5 standard. I am also now playing in a local band and the opportunities for me, both musically and socially, have increased tenfold since learning to play. In addition to this, learning to play the guitar has improved my concentration levels and my patience."

Now take the time to use the blank space on the following page to prepare your own response to this question.

YOUR RESPONSE TO THIS QUESTION

Q7 – Tell me about a time when you have taken it upon yourself to learn a new skill or develop an existing one?

Q8 – Tell me about a time when you changed how you did something in response to feedback from someone else?

How to structure your response:

- What did you need to develop?

- What feedback did you receive and from whom?

- What steps did you take to improve yourself or someone else?

- What did you specifically say or do?

- What was the result?

Strong response

As a police officer you will receive feedback from your supervisory manager (Sergeant) on a regular basis. In their quest to continually improve, the police force will invest time, finances and resources into your development. Part of the learning process includes being able to accept feedback and also being able to improve as a result of it. Strong performing candidates will be able to provide a specific example of where they have taken feedback from an employer or otherwise, and used it to improve themselves.

Weak response

Those candidates who are unable to accept feedback from others and change as a result will generally provide a weak response to this type of question. They will fail to grasp the importance of feedback and in particular where it lies in relation to continuous improvement. Their response will be generic in nature and there will be no real substance or detail to their answer.

Sample response

"During my last appraisal, my line manager identified that I needed to improve in a specific area. I work as a call handler for a large independent communications company. Part of my role involves answering a specific number of calls per hour. If I do not reach my target then this does not allow the company to meet its standards. I found that I was falling behind on the number of calls answered and this was identified during the appraisal. I needed to develop my skills in the manner in which I handled the call. My line manager played back a number of recorded calls that I had dealt with and it was apparent that I was taking too long speaking to the customer about issues that were irrelevant to the call itself. Because I am conscien-

tious and caring person I found myself asking the customer how they were and what kind of day they were having. Despite the customers being more than pleased with level of customer care, this approach was not helping the company and therefore I needed to change my approach. I immediately took on-board the comments of my line manager and also took up the offer of development and call handling training. After the training, which took two weeks to complete, I was meeting my targets with ease This in turn helped the company to reach it's call handling targets."

Now take the time to use the blank space on the following page to prepare your own response to this question.

YOUR RESPONSE TO THIS QUESTION

Q8 – Tell me about a time when you changed how you did something in response to feedback from someone else?

Q9 – Tell me about a time when you noticed a member of your team or group behaving in a manner which was inconsistent with the teams, groups, or organisation's values?

How to structure your answer:

- What was the situation?
- How was the behaviour inconsistent with the team's or organisation's values?
- Why were the colleagues behaving in that way?
- What did you say or do when you noticed this behaviour?
- What difficulties did you face?
- What was the result?

Strong response

Police officers need to have the confidence and ability to challenge unacceptable behaviour whilst at work. In order to understand what unacceptable behaviour is, you first need to know what the values of the organisation are. Candidates who provide a strong response will have a clear understanding of an organisation's values and also how to tackle unacceptable behaviour in the correct manner.

Weak response

Weak responses are generally where a candidate is unaware of the importance of an organisation's values and how they impact on the needs of a team or group. They will not have the confidence to challenge inappropriate behaviour and they will turn a blind eye whenever possible. Their response will lack structure and it will be generic in nature.

Sample response

"Whilst working as a sales person for my previous employer, I was serving a lady who was from an ethnic background. I was helping her to choose a gift for her son's 7th birthday when a group of four youths entered the shop and began looking around at the goods we had for sale. For some strange reason they began to make racist jokes and comments to the lady. I was naturally offended by the comments and was concerned for the lady to whom these comments were directed. Any form of bullying and harassment is not welcome in any situation and I was determined to stop it immediately and protect the lady from any more harm.

The lady was clearly upset by their actions and I too found them both offensive and insensitive. I decided to take immediate action and stood between the lady and the youths to try to protect her from any more verbal abuse or comments. I told them in a calm manner that their comments were not welcome and would not be tolerated. I then called over my manager for assistance and asked him to call the police before asking the four youths to leave the shop. I wanted to diffuse the situation as soon as possible, being constantly aware of the lady's feelings. I was confident that the shop's CCTV cameras would have picked up the four offending youths and that the police would be able to deal with the situation. After the youths had left the shop I sat the lady down and made her a cup of tea whilst we waited for the police to arrive. I did everything that I could to support and comfort the lady and told her that I would be prepared to act as a witness to the racial bullying and harassment that I had just witnessed.

I believe the people acted as they did because of a lack of understanding, education and awareness. Unless people are educated and understand why these comments are not acceptable, then they are not open to change. They behave in this manner because they are unaware of how dangerous their comments and actions are. They believe it is socially acceptable to act this way, when it certainly isn't.

I also feel strongly that if I had not acted and challenged the behaviour the consequences would be numerous. To begin with I would have been condoning this type of behaviour and missing an opportunity to let the offenders know that their actions are wrong (educating them). I would have also been letting the lady down, which would have in turn made her feel frightened, hurt and unsupported. We all have the opportunity to help stop discriminatory behaviour, and providing we ourselves are not in any physical danger, then we should take positive action to stop it."

Now take the time to use the blank space on the following page to prepare your own response to this question.

YOUR RESPONSE TO THIS QUESTION

Q9 – Tell me about a time when you noticed a member of your team or group behaving in a manner which was inconsistent with the teams, groups, or organisation's values?

The next competency we will look at deals with Service Delivery. Let's quickly remind ourselves what this competency covers:

Understands the organisation's objectives and priorities, and how own work fits into these. Plans and organises tasks effectively, taking a structured and methodical approach to achieving outcomes. Manages multiple tasks effectively by thinking things through in advance, prioritising and managing time well. Focuses on the outcomes to be achieved, working quickly and accurately and seeking guidance when appropriate.

Q10 – Can you provide an example of when you have carried out a task in a methodical manner?

How to structure your response:

- What was the task and how did you approach it?

- Were there any rules or instructions that you had to follow?

- What did you do to complete the work as directed?

- What was the result?

- How did you feel about completing the task in this way?

Strong response

Police officers must be able to prioritise tasks and carry them out in a methodical and organised manner in order to achieve the end result. Strong candidates will provide a specific response to this question which details how they went about tackling the situation in a planned and time efficient manner.

Weak response

Weak responses are generic in nature and will demonstrate to the interviewer that the candidate is incapable of delivering an effective service.

Sample response

"Yes, I can. In my current job as car mechanic for a well-known company, I was presented with a difficult and pressurised situation that required me to work unsupervised in a fast, methodical and safe manner.

A member of the team had made a mistake and had fitted a number of wrong components to a car. The car in question was due to be picked up at 2pm and the customer had stated how important it was that his car was ready on time because he had an important meeting to attend. We only had two hours in which to resolve the issue and I volunteered to be the one who would carry out the work on the car.

The problem was that we had three other customers in the workshop waiting for their cars too, so I was the only person who could be spared at that particular time. I started out by looking at the task in a methodical manner and put a plan together that would enable me to complete each task within a set timescale. I then set about my work solidly for the next two hours, making sure that I meticulously carried out each task in line with our operating procedures and my training. I completed the task just before 2pm. I managed to achieve everything that I set out to achieve, whilst following strict safety procedures and regulations.

I understand that the role of a police officer will require me to work under extreme pressure at times and I believe I have the experience to achieve this. I am very meticulous in my work and always ensure that I take personal responsibility to keep up-to-date with procedures and policies in my current job."

Now take the time to use the blank space on the following page to prepare your own response to this question.

YOUR RESPONSE TO THIS QUESTION

Q10 – Can you provide an example of when you have carried out a task in a methodical manner?

Q11 – Can you provide an example of when you have planned or organised an event?

How to structure your response:

- What was the event and how did you approach it?

- What did you consider during the planning or organising stage?

- What did you do to make sure the event went according to plan?

- What was the end result?

- How did you feel about planning and organising it in this way?

Strong response

As a police officer you will undoubtedly be required to plan and prioritise tasks. A simple example of this will be with regards to how you plan your own working day. You will be expected to plan your own time and make sure that all tasks are completed to a high standard, and on time. Make sure your response to this question demonstrates your ability to plan, organise and prioritise tasks. You should also focus on delivering your response in a structured and logical manner.

Weak response

Weak responses are generic in nature and will demonstrate to the interviewer that the candidate is incapable of planning or organising.

Sample response

"A couple of months ago I decided to raise some money for a local children's charity. I read an article in my newspaper which detailed how the charity were looking to raise money in order to purchase some much needed items of equipment that would help to improve disabled children's lives.

I immediately set about thinking of different ways to help and soon decided that a car wash event would be an ideal way to raise some money for them fast. I sat down and created an action plan that detailed what I was going to do and by when. The plan including things such as where I would hold the event, what day the event would take place, who I would recruit to help me out, sponsors, equipment needed and public liability insurance etc. I soon realised there was a lot of work required to pull off the event, so I set myself strict deadlines to meet.

I prioritised the tasks in a logical manner and soon found a venue and date for the event to take place. I contacted my local supermarket and they agreed to help me out by providing the venue, a date for the event to take place on a Saturday, their busiest day, and also public liability insurance for the event. Once I had the venue and date arranged I then needed to recruit helpers for the day. I wrote to all of my neighbours and posted messages on Facebook encouraging people to volunteer and help out – I was soon inundated with volunteers. In addition to this I wrote to the local media to seek their help in promoting the charity event.

The next stage of the planning process was to hold a meeting with the volunteers so that I could brief them on my plan for the day and explain how the event would run. This was also a good time for me to allocate tasks to different members of the team based on their strengths.

The event took place on the intended date and it was a thorough success. To my surprise, we managed to raise over £2,000 for the local charity. I believe the success of the event was entirely down to how I planned it from the get go."

Now take the time to use the blank space on the following page to prepare your own response to this question.

YOUR RESPONSE TO THIS QUESTION

Q11 – Can you provide an example of when you have planned or organised an event?

The next competency we will look at deals with Public Service. Let's quickly remind ourselves what this competency covers:

Demonstrates a real belief in public service, focusing on what matters to the public and will best serve their interests. Understands the expectations, changing needs and concerns of different communities, and strives to address them. Builds public confidence by talking with people in local communities to explore their viewpoints and break down barriers between them and the police. Understands the impact and benefits of policing for different communities, and identifies the best way to deliver services to them. Works in partnership with other agencies to deliver the best possible overall service to the public.

Q12 – Can you provide an example when you have provided excellent service to an individual or group?

How to structure your response:

- What was the service that was being delivered?

- What did you consider when dealing with the individual or group?

- Were there any special requirements you needed to take into consideration?

- What was the outcome?

- How did you feel about delivering the service in the way that you did?

Strong response

The police force is a public service and police officers need to be able to provide a high level of focused service. Strong responses to this question will provide evidence of where the candidate focused on the needs of the customer and worked hard to achieve a successful outcome.

Weak response

Weak responses are generic in nature and will demonstrate to the interviewer that the candidate is incapable of delivering high quality service.

Sample response

"Whilst working as a shop assistant in my current role, a member of the public came in to complain about a pair of football shoes that he had bought for

his son's birthday. When his son came to open the present on the morning of his birthday, he noticed that one of the football boots was a larger size than the other. He was supposed to be playing football with his friends that morning and wanted to wear his new boots. However, due to the shop's mistake, this was not possible.

Naturally, the boy was very upset. I remained calm throughout and listened to the gentleman very carefully, showing complete empathy for his son's situation. This immediately defused any potential confrontation. I then told him how sorry I was for the mistake that had happened, and that I would feel exactly the same if it was my own son who it had happened to. I then told the gentleman that I would refund the money in full and give his son a new pair of football boots to the same value as the previous pair. The man was delighted with my offer. Not only that, I then offered to give the man a further discount of 10% on any future purchase, due to the added inconvenience that was caused by him having to return to the shop to sort out the problem. In order to achieve a successful outcome I used exceptional communication skills and remained calm throughout. The potential for losing a customer was averted by my actions and I feel sure the man would return to our shop again in the future. I am a strong believer in delivering high quality customer service and can be relied upon to be a positive role model for the police force if I am to be successful."

Now take the time to use the blank space on the following page to prepare your own response to this question.

YOUR RESPONSE TO THIS QUESTION

Q12 – Can you provide an example when you have provided excellent service to an individual or group?

Q13 – Can you give an example when you have responded to the changing needs of an individual or group of people?

How to structure your response:

- What was the situation you were required to deal with?

- What did you consider when dealing with the individual or group?

- What was the 'need' you had to respond to and also what did you decide to take into consideration?

- What was the outcome?

- How did you feel about responding to the need in the way that you did?

Strong response

The police force is a public service and police officers need to be able to provide a high level of focused service. Strong responses to this question will provide evidence of where the candidate focused on the changing 'needs' of the individual or group and worked hard to achieve a successful outcome, which they approved of.

Weak response

Weak responses are generic in nature and will demonstrate to the interviewer that the candidate is incapable of delivering high quality service.

Sample response

"Whilst working as a team leader at a children's day care nursery, a couple arrived one morning to enquire about space for their two young children. The couple were new to the area and their English was very poor. They had only recently moved to England and were originally from China. Communication was extremely difficult but I was very keen to help them and was determined to meet their needs. The nursery was not ideally setup to cater for people from different countries, simply because all of our staff were English speaking. However, I decided to change things and immediately sought permission from the nursery owners to pay for a telephone interpreter so that we could establish the couple's needs and ascertain what level of service we could offer them. Whilst the couple were at the centre I managed to source an interpreter by searching on the Internet. Using the company credit card, which my manager had agreed to, I paid for a 10 minute interpretation service there and then, and asked the interpreter to ask the couple a number of specific

questions which focused on their needs for their children and the level of service we could offer them. Following the telephone interpretation consultation I managed to ascertain that the couple wanted to drop their children off at set times each day of the week and leave them in our care for a maximum of 4 hours each time, something which we agreed to. We then agreed a mutually convenient start date for their children.

Once the couple had left I then contacted the nursery owner again and persuaded her to allow me to recruit a nursery nurse who could speak Chinese. After explaining the benefits to her, she agreed. I then set about recruiting a member of staff who would be suitable for this role. Whilst it was not easy to find a suitably qualified nursery nurse with the appropriate language skills, I did eventually manage to find someone in time for when the couple's children started with us and the outcome was a successful one."

Now take the time to use the blank space on the following page to prepare your own response to this question.

YOUR RESPONSE TO THIS QUESTION

Q13 – Can you give an example when you have responded to the changing needs of an individual or group of people?

Q14 – Can you give an example when you have broken down barriers between individuals or a group of people?

How to structure your response:

- What were the barriers you were required to break down?

- What did you consider when dealing with the individuals or group?

- What did you decide to take into consideration when breaking down the barriers?

- What was the outcome?

- How did you feel about dealing with the situation in the way that you did?

Strong response

As a police officer you will need to break down barriers between communities and the police force. Achieving this takes courage, skill, determination and resilience. Strong responses provide specific examples of where an individual has been committed to breaking down barriers, despite any setbacks or difficulties.

Weak response

Weak responses are generic in nature and will demonstrate to the interviewer that the candidate is incapable of breaking down barriers between individuals or groups.

Sample response

"Whilst working in a large warehouse as a factory worker I was acutely aware of tensions between different workers. These tensions had been on going for a number of years. I believed the tensions centred on a breakdown in communication between different groups of people who worked at the warehouse. In particular, there were tensions between white male workers and Asian male workers. I decided that something needed to be done, and so set about speaking to people within the different groups to see what the issues were and whether there was any desire within the groups to break down these barriers once and for all. After speaking to key members of each group of workers I came to the conclusion that the main reason for the barriers was simply down to a lack of understanding and respect.

In order to improve relations between the groups I asked my manager for permission to hold a teambuilding day. I explained to him the benefits of investing time and money into breaking down the barriers between the groups of men and he wholeheartedly agreed that it was a positive idea. I was aware of a company, situated not too far from the factory that ran these types of days. I then arranged a date for the teambuilding day to take place and informed all members of staff of the event and how they could take part. The teambuilding day would consist of different group events that were designed to build morale, improve communications and encourage team spirit.

On the day of the event I had pre-arranged for people from the two groups to be on different teams, so as to encourage them to start mixing with each other and communicating more effectively. As soon as the first event started I sensed an improvement in relations and communication between the men. This was immensely satisfying to see. Once the teambuilding day was over I had arranged for everyone to attend a local restaurant where they would all sit down together and socialise in a relaxed manner in order to continue the good work which had taken place during the day.

Everyone agreed that the teambuilding day had been a great success and the following day at work the atmosphere had improved considerably. A few weeks later my manager called me in to his office to congratulate me on the event. He informed me that productivity within the factory had increased by 20% and he attributed the increase to my efforts in breaking down the barriers between the factory workers."

Now take the time to use the blank space on the following page to prepare your own response to this question.

YOUR RESPONSE TO THIS QUESTION

Q14 – Can you give an example when you have broken down barriers between individuals or a group of people?

INTERVIEW QUESTIONS AND ANSWERS FOR THE POLICE OFFICER FINAL INTERVIEW

INTERVIEW QUESTIONS AND ANSWERS FOR THE POLICE OFFICER FINAL INTERVIEW

Some police forces have started to introduce what is called a final interview. The final interview is in addition to the assessment centre competency-based interview and will take on a different format.

Within this section of the guide I have provided you with some insider tips and advice on how to prepare for the interview, the type of questions that you may be asked and also how to respond to them. I have also provided you with space after many of the questions in which I would like you to formulate your own response based on your experiences and research. This will be excellent practice for the interview, so please take the time to construct your own answers.

To begin with, let's take a look at a few more details relating to the final interview.

About the interview

The interview will usually take place at the force's training centre or a similar establishment. The purpose of the final interview is to allow the force to ask you questions that are outside of the competencies that have been assessed at the assessment centre. In essence it allows the force to find out more about you, your application, your motivations for wanting to become a police officer, and what you know about the role and the force that you are applying to join. They may also ask you questions that are based around what you might do in a given situation.

The interview panel will normally consist of 2-3 people and is usually made up of uniformed police officers and also a member of the human resources team. The length of the interview will very much depend on the questions the panel want to ask you and also how long your responses are. In general terms the interview will normally last for approximately one hour.

How to prepare for the final interview

If you have made it this far in the selection process then you have done tremendously well. The Police Force is certainly interested in recruiting you but they want to find out more about you first. There are a number of areas that you will need to prepare for and these are as follows:

1. Interview technique.

2. The reasons why you want to become a police officer and what you know about the role.

3. Application form.

4. What you know about the force you are applying to join.

5. Situational interview questions.

Now that we understand how to prepare for the interview, let us break down each particular section in detail.

Interview technique

Many candidates spend little or no time improving or developing their interview technique. It is important that you spend sufficient time on this area, as it will allow your confidence to improve.

The way to improve interview technique is to carry out what we call a mock interview. Mock interviews are where you ask a friend or relative to ask you a number of interview questions under formalised interview conditions. This can be achieved at home across your dining room table or even whilst sat on the chairs in your living room.

During the mock interview you should work on your interview technique. The mock interview will also give you a valuable opportunity to try out your responses to a number of sample interview questions that are contained within this guide. It is important that your mock interviewer provides you with constructive feedback. Do not choose somebody who will tell you that you were great, even when you weren't, as this just defeats the whole purpose of a mock interview.

Carrying out a mock interview

- Choose a quiet room in the house or at another suitable location.

- Set the room up with a table and two chairs.

- The interviewer then invites you into the room and the interview commences. Don't forget to be polite and courteous to the interviewer and only sit down when invited to do so.

- When the interviewer asks you the questions, respond to them in a logical manner and in a tone of voice that can be easily heard.

- Throughout the mock interview work hard on your technique and style.

Sit upright at all times and look at the interviewer using soft eye contact. Do not fidget or slouch in the interview chair.

- Once the interview is over, ask the interviewer for feedback on your performance.

- Repeat the process at least three times until you are comfortable with your technique and style of answering.

The reasons why you want to become a police officer and what you know about the role

During the final interview the panel may ask you questions that relate to why you want to become a police officer and in particular what you know about the role.

Why do you want to become a police officer?

In the build-up to your interview you need to think carefully about why you want to become a police officer and what it is exactly that has attracted you to the role. Those candidates who want to become a police officer so that they can 'catch criminals' and 'ride about in a police car with the blue lights flashing' will score poorly. Only you will know the exact reasons why you want to join the police but here are some examples of good reasons, and examples of poor reasons.

Good reasons to give

- To make a difference to your community, make it a safer place and reduce any fear that the public may have.

- To carry out a job that is worthwhile and one that makes a difference.

- The variety of the job and the different challenges that you will face on a day-to-day basis.

- The chance to work with a highly professional team that is committed to achieving the values and principles of the force.

- The opportunity to learn new skills.

Poor reasons to give

- The pay and pension.

- The leave or holiday that you will get.

- Wearing a uniform, which ultimately means you don't have to pay for your own work clothes.

- Catching criminals and driving a police car.

What do you know about the role?

After studying this guide you will know a considerable amount about the role of a police officer. Before the final interview you must carry out plenty of research into the role and what the force will expect of you as a serving police officer.

Remember that the role is predominantly based around the core competencies, so be fully familiar with them before you attend the interview. It is also advisable that you study the 'Police Could You?' website, your recruitment literature, and also the website of the force you are applying to join.

Application form

During the final interview the panel may ask you questions that relate to your application form. In a previous section of this guide we advised you to make sure you photocopy your application form prior to sending it off.

Before you attend the final interview familiarise yourself with the contents of your form and be prepared for any questions that you may be asked relating to it.

What you know about the force you are applying to join

During the final interview there is a strong possibility that you will be asked questions that relate to the force you are applying to join.

The following sample questions are the types that have been asked during final interviews in the past:

Q. What is it that has attracted you to this particular force?

If you live in the county area then this will be relatively easy to respond to. Have a good understanding of your local community and the problems that it faces. I also recommend you visit the website of the force you are applying to join. Find out what pro-active measures they are taking in their fight against crime and use it in your response. Here's a good response to this question:

"Having lived in the county for many years I am already familiar with the good work the force carries out. I am constantly reading about the good news sto-

ries the police are carrying out in the local community and I want to be part of the organisation. Not only am I impressed with the local, pro-active initiatives that are being carried out but I am also want to be a part of an organisation that cares about the work it does. During my research I also noticed that the force encourages members of the public to talk online to their local police officers. I think this is a fantastic way of encouraging the local community to build relationships with the police, as this in turn builds trust and enables the officers to gather intelligence and vital information in their work against crime in the community."

Q. What can you tell me about the structure of this force?

Visit the force's website to find out more about the structure and make-up of the organisation you are wishing to join.

Q. What can you tell me about the geographical area of this police force?

You can find out this information by spending time on the police force website. In addition to this there is also nothing to stop you from visiting your local police station and requesting information on the geographical layout of the force. The best people to gain this information from are your local police officers and police community support officers.

Q. Can you tell me how this force is doing in relation to crime reduction?

You can find out this information on the forces website. A word of warning though, if the force is not doing particularly well in a specific area do not repeat any negative press stories during the interview. Always focus on the positive work they are doing. For example, whilst being by the television cameras immediately following a fire, I would always put a positive spin on the story. If we had lost 80% of the building to fire, I would never actually state this during the television interview. Instead, I would say something like:

"Fire crews worked extremely hard throughout the night to fight the fire. They carried out some excellent work and they managed to save 20% of the building."

This sounds much better than saying we lost 80%!

Q. What crime reduction activities is this force currently involved in?

Again, you can find this out on the forces website. I would also recommend visiting:

www.police.uk

Q. What is neighbourhood policing and how does this force approach it?

Neighbourhood Policing is provided by teams of police officers and Police Community Support Officers (PCSOs) in each individual force, often together with Special Constables, local authority wardens, volunteers and partners. There are now 3,600 Neighbourhood Policing Teams (NPTs) across the UK. Local Policing aims to provide people who live or work in a neighbourhood with:

Access - to local policing services through a named point of contact

Influence - over policing priorities in their neighbourhood

Interventions - joint action with partners & the public

Answers - sustainable solutions & feedback on what is being done

This means that neighbourhood teams:

- Publicise how to get in touch with them

- Find out what the local issues are that make people feel unsafe in their neighbourhood and ask them to put them in order of priority

- Decide with partners and local people what should be done to deal with those priorities and work with them to deliver the solutions

- Let people know what is being done and find out if they are satisfied with the results.

Q. What are the ambitions of this police force?

You can find out this information on the website of the force you are applying to join. For example, my local police force is Kent. On their website they publish a 3 year plan which sets out their plans and objectives for the forthcoming 3 yearly period. At the time of writing, their plans include:

Priorities	Objectives
Delivering effective local policing	Reducing crime and effectively dealing with anti-social behaviour; Improving visibility, accessibility and responsiveness; Improving public satisfaction; Bringing offenders to justice.
Protecting the public from serious harm	Protecting the public from serious and organised crime.
Making best use of our resources	Demonstrating increasing efficiency and value for money.

Q. Who are our partners and stakeholders?

In general, the stakeholders and partners of the police include:

- Communities within the police force area, including those who are not resident but work or travel within the county.

- Police Authority; Government Office for the area, MEPs, MPs, Independent Advisory Groups; Special Interest Groups, County, Borough/District councils/councillors; Community Safety Partnerships; Local Criminal Justice Board; Unions and Staff Associations; County/Regional media organisations; 3rd party organisations; Neighbourhood Watch and Business Watch.

- Fire and Rescue Service, Ambulance Service, Local Authority, Coastguard, CCTV groups, Environmental Agency.

- Police staff, Police officers, Specials, SPOCs and volunteers.

In order to prepare for questions that relate to the force you are applying to join, your first port of call is their website. From here you will be able to find out a considerable amount of information about their structure and activities, including the policing pledge and their success in driving down crime.

You may also wish to consider contacting your local police station and asking if it is possible to talk to a serving police officer about his or her role and the activities that the force are currently engaged in.

Situational interview questions

During the final interview the panel may ask you questions that relate to how you would respond or act in a given situation. This type of question is called a 'situational' type question.

Your response to each situational question must be 'specific' in nature. This means that you must provide an example where you have already been in this type of situation. During your response you should provide details of how you handled or dealt with the situation, preferably with a successful outcome.

Do not fall into the trap of providing a 'generic' response that details what you 'would do' if the situation arose, unless of course you have not been in this type of situation before.

When responding to situational questions try to structure your responses in a logical and concise manner. The way to achieve this is to use the 'STAR' method of interview question response construction:

Situation

Start off your response to the interview question by explaining what the 'situation' was and who was involved.

Task

Once you have detailed the situation, explain what the 'task' was, or what needed to be done.

Action

Now explain what 'action' you took, and what action others took. Also explain why you took this particular course of action.

Result

Finally explain what the outcome or result was following your actions and those of others. Try to demonstrate in your response that the result was positive because of the action you took.

Finally, explain to the panel what you would do differently if the same situation arose again. It is good to be reflective at the end of your responses. This demonstrates a level of maturity and it will also show the panel that you are willing to learn from every experience.

Now that we have looked into how to prepare for the final interview, it is time to provide you with a number of sample questions and answers. Please note that the questions provided here are for practice purposes only and are not to be relied upon to be the exact questions that you will be asked during your final interview.

Sample final interview questions and sample responses

Sample question number 1

Tell us why you want to become a police officer?

Sample response

"I have worked in my current role now for a number of years. I have an excellent employer and enjoy working for them but unfortunately no longer find my job challenging. I understand that the role of a police officer is both demanding and rewarding and I believe I have the qualities to thrive in such an environment. I love working under pressure, working as part of a team that is diverse in nature and helping people in difficult situations. The public expectations of the police are very high and I believe I have the right qualities to help the police deliver the right service to the community.

I have studied the police core competencies and believe that I have the skills to match them and deliver what they require."

Top tips

- Don't be negative about your current or previous employer.
- Be positive, enthusiastic and upbeat in your response.
- Make reference to the core competencies if possible.

Use the box that follows to create your own unique response to this question:

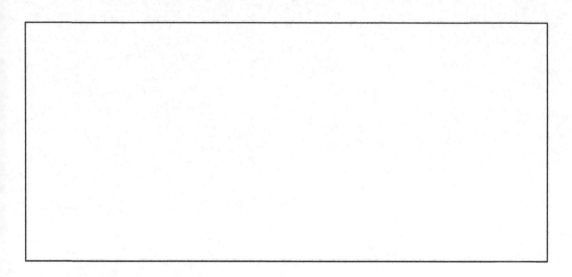

Sample question number 2

Why have you chosen this particular Police Force?

Sample response

"I have carried out extensive research into the Police Service and in particular this force. The level of service it provides has impressed me. The website provides the community with direct access to a different range of topics and the work that is being carried out through your community wardens is impressive. I have looked at the national and local crime statistics and read many different newspapers and articles.

I like this Police Force because of its reputation and the police officers that I have spoken to have told me that they get a great deal of job satisfaction from working here."

Top tips

- Research the force thoroughly and make reference to particular success stories that they have achieved.

- Be positive, enthusiastic and upbeat in your response.

- Be positive about their force and don't be critical of it, even if you think it needs improving in certain areas.

Use the box that follows to create your own unique response to this question:

Sample question number 3

What does the role of a police officer involve?

Sample response

"Before I carried out my research and looked into the role of the police officer, I had the normal, stereotypical view of a police officer in that they catch criminals and reduce crime for a living.

Whilst there is an element of that in the job, the police officer's role is far more diverse and varied. For example, they are there to serve the community and reduce the element of fear. They do this by communicating with their communities and being visual wherever possible.

They may need to pay particular attention to a person or groups of people who are the victims of crime or hatred. Therefore the role of a police officer is to both physically and psychologically protect the community that they are serving.

It is also their role to work with other organisations such as the Fire Service, Social Services and other public sector bodies to try to reduce crime in a coordinated response as opposed to on their own."

Top tips

- Understand the police core competencies and be able to recite them word for word.

- Understand the terms 'community policing' and 'policing pledge'.

Use the box that follows to create your own unique response to this question:

Sample question number 4

If one of the members of your team was gay and they told you this over a cup of tea at work, how do you think you would react?

Sample response

"I would have no problem at all. A person's sexual preference is their right and they should not be treated any differently for this. My attitude towards them and our working relationship would not be affected in any way. I have always treated everyone with respect and dignity at all times and will continue to do so throughout my career."

Top tips

- Understand everything there is to know about equality and fairness. If you do not believe in it then this job is not for you.

- Visit the website **www.gay.police.uk**

Use the box that follows to create your own unique response to this question:

Sample question number 5

If you were given an order that you thought was incorrect would you carry it out?

Sample response

"Yes I would. I would always respect my senior officers and their decisions.

However, if I thought something could be done in a better way, then I do think that it is important to put it across but in a structured and non-confrontational manner. During a debrief would probably be an appropriate time to offer up my views and opinions if asked but I would never refuse to carry out an order or even question it during an operational incident or otherwise."

Top tips

- It is good to say that you would offer suggestions.

- The police force is a disciplined environment; therefore, you will be expected to carry out orders without question.

Use the box that follows to create your own unique response to this question:

Sample question number 6

What do you understand by the term equality and fairness?

Sample response

"It is an unfortunate fact that certain groups in society are still more likely to suffer from unfair treatment and discrimination. It is important for the Police Force and its staff to strive to eliminate all forms of unfair treatment and discrimination on the grounds that are specified in their policies or codes of practice.

Equality and fairness is the working culture in which fair treatment of all is the norm."

Top tips

- Try to read the Police Force's policy on equality and fairness. You may be able to find this by visiting their website or asking them for a copy of it to help you in your preparation.

- Consider reading the Race Relations Act, and understand the duties that are placed upon public sector organisations such as the police.

Use the box that follows to create your own unique response to this question:

Sample question number 7

How do you think the police could recruit more people from ethnic minority groups?

Sample response

"To begin with it is important that Police Forces continue to build effective public relations. This can be achieved through certain avenues such as the force's website or even the local press. If the Police Force has a community liaison officer then this would be a good way to break down any barriers in the communities that we want to recruit from.

Another option is to ask people from these specific groups how they view this Police Force and what they think we could do to recruit more people from their community. Along with this it may be an option to focus media campaigns where there are higher populations of ethnic minority groups."

Top tips

- Have a good knowledge of the police forces equality policy.

- Try and come up with your own ideas for recruiting diverse members of the community.

Use the box that follows to create your own unique response to this question:

More police officer interview questions to prepare for and tips how to respond

Q. Why do you want to become a police officer?

Remember to include in your response things like:

- Having the ability to improve society through pro-active police work

- Protecting the public

- Making a positive difference to the community

- Using your skills and attributes in a positive manner

- The challenge that comes with the role

- Being part of a disciplined and successful organisation

- Being in an organisation where the opportunity for development exists

Use the box that follows to create your own unique response to this question:

```




```

Q. What are your strengths?

Try and provide strengths that are relevant to the role and the core competencies being assessed. The following list contains some recommendations:

- Driven, motivated and enthusiastic
- Determined and persistent
- Organised and capable of keeping an accurate and up-to-date diary
- Mentally and physically fit
- Punctual and reliable
- Able to take, keep and record accurate notes
- Flexible and happy to work shifts/unsociable hours
- Able to identify my weak areas and take steps to improve them
- Always looking for ways to develop and improve
- Calm in a crisis
- Able to work alone and unsupervised
- An ability to defuse difficult situations
- A good listener and communicator
- A great team-worker and someone who fits in well to any team
- A hard worker

Use the box that follows to create your own unique response to this question:

Q. What are your weaknesses?

This question is harder to respond to than the previous one. Here's a sample response to help you:

"I don't have many weaknesses but those that I do have I am aware of and I am taking steps to improve. During the selection process for becoming a police officer I found it difficult to carry out the numerical tests that form part of the initial recruitment test. This is because it has been a long time since I was in education. However, in order to improve in this weak area I started attending night school in order to get some much-needed tuition. I always try to improve on my weaknesses, whatever they are."

Use the box that follows to create your own unique response to this question:

Q. What can you tell us about this particular Police Force?

The following sample response is based on Greater Manchester Police Force at the time of writing:

"Greater Manchester Police was formed in 1974 and it now serves more than 2.5 million people. The approximate area it covers is 500 square miles. The police force is divided into twelve divisions, which are Bolton, Bury, Metropolitan, North Manchester, Oldham, Rochdale, Salford, South Manchester, Stockport, Tameside, Trafford and Wigan. There is also a specialist division based at Manchester International Airport. The main objectives of the force are to carry out effective policing by putting people first in everything they do, being proud of delivering excellent service, working with, and for, the people of Greater Manchester in order to make communities safe and feel safer. Neighbourhood Policing is at the heart of Greater Manchester Police. The main aim is to make Greater Manchester a better place to live, work and play. The force prides itself on having the right people in the right place at the right time, tackling everything from anti-social behaviour and burglary to terrorism and organised crime. During my research I have found out that Greater Manchester each of the twelve divisions has a combination of Neighbourhood Policing Units, each of which is managed by a Neighbourhood Inspector. These units have specific areas of responsibility and consist of smaller, localised, Neighbourhood Policing Teams which include local police officers and Police Community Support Officers. These Neighbourhood Policing Teams have been set up to focus on the needs of the local community. They have regular meetings where members of the public can help set the priorities for their area."

Use the box that follows to create your own unique response to this question based on the force you are applying to join:

Q. What do you understand by the term 'teamwork'?

"In general terms teamwork is the process of working collaboratively with a group of people in order to achieve a goal. Teamwork is often a crucial part of an organisation, as it is often necessary for colleagues to work well together, trying their best in any circumstance. Teamwork means that people will try to cooperate, using their individual skills and providing constructive feedback, despite any personal conflict between individuals. In respect of teamwork in the police force the same applies. Everyone who works in, or for, the police force will work towards the mission and objectives that the force dictates. Within the police force there will be many team members, including call handling staff, police officers, senior managers, police special constables, PCSOs to name just a few. Even the cleaners who maintain the cleanliness of the police stations are an integral part of the team."

Use the box that follows to create your own unique response to this question:

Q. What qualities should a team member have?

There are basically a number of qualities that an individual should have in order to become a competent team member. Here are just a few:

- An ability to work towards the aims and objectives of the team

- An ability to support other team members

- An excellent communicator

- Strength of mind

- Sense of humour

- Reliability

- An ability to listen

- Able to contribute towards the team

- Creativity

- Problem solver

- Respectful of the other team members

- An ability to work with everyone, regardless of who they are or their back
  ground

Use the box that follows to create your own unique response to this question:

```



```

Q. Why would you make a good police officer?

Here's a sample response to this question:

"I believe I would make a good police officer because I have a desire to work within the community and also work towards making it a safer place to live, work and play. I have some great qualities that I believe would help the police force deliver its objectives. To begin with, I always remain calm in a crisis situation and have a confident and resilient approach to my work, whatever it may be. I have a track record for working hard and I have a flexible nature. I also have some experience of working unsociable hours

so I know that this part of the job will not be a problem to me. I also have exceptional organisational skills and can be relied upon to keep accurate records whenever required. Finally I am a very good team worker and enjoy working with people from different backgrounds."

Use the box that follows to create your own unique response to this question:

Q. If you saw a colleague being bullied or harassed, what would you do?

No form of bullying or harassment should ever be tolerated, not only in the workplace but also in the community. Here's a sample response to assist you during your preparation:

"The first thing I would do is intervene and stop it. I strongly believe that there is no place in the workplace and society for bullying or harassment. I would remain calm and intervene without physical force or aggression. If necessary, I would try and act as a mediator between the two parties with a view to resolving the issue. If I believed that either party were in serious danger then I would report the incident to my line manager immediately."

Use the box that follows to create your own unique response to this question:

Q. What do you think the qualities of an effective police officer are?

"I believe the qualities include trust, determination, integrity, reliability, being community-focused, a great team-worker, a good communicator, caring, resilient, confident, physically and mentally fit, organised, punctual, an ability to keep accurate notes and records and also being a positive role model."

Use the box that follows to create your own unique response to this question:

Q. What have you done so far to find out about the role of a police officer?

"I have spent lots of time learning and understanding the core competencies that are relevant to the role. I did this because I wanted to be fully 100% sure that I could carry out the role, and I believe that I can. I have spent time studying the police force website in order to learn about the geographical area and also how the force interacts with the members of the community in which it serves. I have also studied the three-year community plan that the force has published. It was important for me to read this document, as I understand that I would have to work towards these important goals if I am to be successful. I have also visited my local police station and spent time talking to the local officers about their work. Finally, I attended a local neighbourhood watch meeting in my parish area. This was a great insight into the work the force carries out. I now fully understand how committed the police force is to improving the community."

Use the box that follows to create your own unique response to this question:

Q. Give an example of when you have had to work as a team.

"I have had lots of experience to date working as part of a team. In my current role as a bricklayer I have been working on a project with many other skilled

workers and labourers. The project involves building ten new houses within a three-month period. We are now half way through the project and it is running smoothly and on time.

During this particular project I have been required to work with people who I did not know before the start of the build. This has not been a problem for me, as I have not issue with working with anyone, regardless of who they are. I always start off by introducing myself to the rest of the team and ask the other team-members to introduce themselves. This acts as a bit of an icebreaker and it gets everyone talking. At the start of each working day we listen carefully to the brief provided by the foreman. As we work through the tasks set by the foreman we communicate with each other clearly so that everyone knows what is going on and whereabouts we all are with the project. If anyone in the building team starts to slow up we all gather round to help him or her catch up. As a team member I am always focused on the end goal and work very hard to carry out my job meticulously and diligently."

Use the box that follows to create your own unique response to this question:

Q. What would you do if a member of your team was not pulling their weight or doing their job effectively?

"I would first of all ask them if there was anything wrong, or if there was anything I could do to support them. The member of the team might be

having personal issues, and if this were the case, I would want to support them and help them through it. If it were simply a case of them being lazy, then I would take action to stop it. I would take them to one side and tactfully point out to them how important their role was within the team. I would inform them that without their full attention on the task in hand we would not be able to achieve our goal."

Use the box that follows to create your own unique response to this question:

Q. Have you ever had to diffuse a confrontational situation? What did you do and what did you say?

Before creating a response to this question, consider the following:

1. One of the core competencies includes the ability to act with resilience. You must be capable of defusing confrontational situations in a calm and confident manner.

2. When dealing with this type of situation you should never become confrontational or aggressive yourself.

Now take a look at the following sample response to the question:

"Yes I have, on a number of occasions. Whilst working in my current role as a shop manager I had to defuse a confrontational situation with an angry

customer. The customer was not happy with the service he had received and he wanted to complain. I started listening to his concerns, but as he progressed with his complaint, he became angrier and confrontational to the point that I had to intervene. Whilst listening to him I detected that his voice was becoming more aggressive. I very calmly and politely intervened. I asked him to cease from using threatening language and explained to him that I was here to help him but that I would not tolerate abusive language. I also asked him to come to the rear of the shop so that we would be out of the way of the other customers. When we arrived at the rear of the shop I quietly explained that I understood his concerns and that I would do all that I could to resolve them, but in return he had to remain calm and not become confrontational. My approach worked. He apologised for his actions and carried on detailing his complaint in a calm manner. I believe it is important to be calm, yet firm when dealing with situations of this nature."

Use the box that follows to create your own unique response to this question:

```

```

Q. What are the main issues affecting the police at this current time?

This question is designed to see how up-to-date you are with current affairs and issues affecting the police force in your area. The following sample response is relevant at the time of writing.

"The main issue affecting the police force at present is the restriction is budget that I understand has been placed by the Local Authority. This means

the police force must work harder to deliver efficiency savings and therefore make the service better value for money. This may mean that police officers will be required to carry out extra duties, but ultimately, they will need to work more efficiently. Other issues affecting the police include the constant drive to reduce crime in the local area and to make the community a safer place to live, work and play."

Q. What do you understand about the term 'equality and diversity'?

Equality is the current term for 'Equal Opportunities'. It is based on the legal obligation to comply with anti-discrimination legislation. Equality protects people from being discriminated against on the grounds of group membership i.e. sex, race disability, sexual orientation, religion, belief, or age.

Diversity implies a wide range of conditions and characteristics. In terms of organisations and their workforces it is about valuing and reaping the benefits of a varied workforce that makes the best of people's talents whatever their backgrounds.

Diversity encompasses visible and non-visible individual differences. It can be seen in the makeup of your workforce in terms of gender, ethnic minorities, disabled people etc., about where those people are in terms of management positions, job opportunities, terms and conditions in the workplace. Diversity is about respecting individual differences, and people's differences can be many and varied:

- Race
- Culture
- National origin
- Region
- Gender
- Sexual Orientation
- Age
- Marital Status
- Politics
- Religion
- Ethnicity

- Disability
- Socio-economic differences
- Family structure
- Health
- Values

Embracing equality and diversity brings to an organisation a wide range of experience, ideas and creativity whilst giving the individual employee a feeling of being enabled to work to their full potential.

Combined together, equality and diversity drive an organisation to comply with anti-discrimination legislation as well as emphasising the positive benefits of diversity such as drawing on a wider pool of talent, positively motivating all employees and meeting the needs of a wider customer base.

Employers such as the police force are now encouraged to deepen and enrich their "equal opportunities" policies and strategies into an encompassing Equality and Diversity policy with a strategy and action plans that managers, workers and other stakeholders can contribute to and benefit from.

Use the box that follows to create your own unique response to this question:

Q. If you ever heard a racist or sexist remark at work, what would you do?

"I would stop it immediately. No form of abuse should be tolerated. I would intervene in a safe and calm manner. I would also ensure that this behaviour was reported to my line manager so that further action could be considered."

Use the box that follows to create your own unique response to this question:

Q. How do you think you would cope with working the police shift system?

Working unsociable hours is part and parcel of life in the police force. I worked shifts in the Fire Service for 17 years and it can take its toll after a while. You need to be 100% certain that you can cope with the irregular shift patterns and that your family supports you. Take a look at the following sample response:

"I believe I would cope very well. I have taken into consideration the fact that I would be required to work unsociable hours and I am prepared for this. I have discussed it with my family and I have their full support. I have worked office based hours for many years now and I am actually looking forward to the change."

Use the box that follows to create your own unique response to this question:

Final tips and advice for preparing for the final interview

- The Police may ask you more generic questions relating to your past experiences or skills. These may be in relation to solving problems, working as an effective team member, dealing with difficult or aggressive people and diffusing confrontational situations. Make sure you have examples for each of these.

- Try to speak to current serving police officers of the force that you are applying to join. Ask them what it is like to work for that particular force and what the current policing issues are. From their feedback take the positive points but don't use any detrimental or negative feedback during the interview.

- Try to think of a time when you have made a mistake and how you learnt from the experience. It is always good to say that you 'reflect' on your actions and take necessary steps to improve for next time.

- When you complete the application form make sure you keep a copy of it. Before you go to your interview ensure that you read the application form over and over again as you may find you are asked questions about your responses.

- Don't be afraid to ask the interviewer to repeat a question if you do not hear it the first time. Take your time when answering and be measured in your responses.

- If you don't know the answer to a question then be honest and just say 'I don't know'. This is far better than trying to answer a question that you have no knowledge about. Conversely, if your answer to a question is challenged there is nothing wrong with sticking to your point but make sure you acknowledge the interviewer's thoughts or views. Be polite and never get into a debate.

-You will be scored against the current police core competencies so make sure you try to structure your answers accordingly. The police core competencies are the first thing you should learn during your preparation.

Frequently asked questions relating to the final interview

Q. How long will my interview last?

A. Of course this very much depends on how long your responses are.

Generally the interview will last between 45 and 60 minutes.

Top tips

- Make sure you drink plenty of water the day before the interview. This will help your mind to stay focused and also keep you hydrated during your interview.

- Avoid alcohol the day before the interview and certainly do not have a drink the day of the interview. Whilst this may help to calm your nerves, the panel will be able to smell alcohol on your breath.

Q. Do you think I should ask questions at the end of my interview?

A. This can't do any harm providing that the questions aren't inappropriate or harmful to your chances of success. Questions such as "Thank you for taking the time to interview me, can you tell me what the next stage is please?" are satisfactory questions.

However, questions such as "I have read that the Police Force in this area have been criticised for their poor crime reduction figures lately, what are they going to do about it?" are definitely not advised. Do not try to be clever!

Top tips

- Be smart. Tidy hair, clean shoes, suit etc. all create a good image. Also spend time sitting upright in a chair at home and pretend that you are being interviewed.

- Carry out a mock interview prior to your actual interview day.

- When answering your questions respond to the panel as opposed to the person who has asked you the question.

- Make eye contact with the members of the panel as opposed to looking at the floor. However, don't be aggressive in your eye contact.

Q. Is it okay to use 'body language' during my interview to express myself?

A. Yes, most definitely.

Using your hands or facial expression during any interview is a positive aspect as it demonstrates confidence. However, there is a fine line between subtle expression and overdoing it. If it becomes too obvious then it can be off-putting for the panel. Try sitting in front of a mirror and practise saying the reasons why you want to become a police officer. This will give you an idea of what the panel will be looking at during your interview.

Top tips

- Sit upright in the chair at all times and do not slouch.

- Smile whenever possible and be confident.

- Rest the palms of your hands on your knees when you are not using them to express yourself and keep your feet flat on the ground.

Q. What are the scoring criteria for the final police officer interview?

A. Don't get tied down or concerned with specific pass marks or pass rates.

The police will score you using their own criteria. Where possible, try to structure your responses to the interview questions around the core competencies.

You may find some of the following phrases useful when constructing your answers:

- Dignity and respect;

- Team working;

- Strong working relationships;

- Effective team member;

- Achieving common goals;

- Customer focus;

- Community policing;

- Policing pledge;

- Sensitive to cultural issues;

- Sensitive towards racial differences;

- Presenting the right image to the public;

- Effective communication;

- Identify problems and make effective decisions;

- Motivated, conscientious and committed;

- Calm, considerate and can work well under pressure.

Visit www.how2become.com to find more titles and courses that will help you to pass the police officer selection process:

- Online police officer testing
- 1-day police officer training course
- Police officer books and DVD's
- Psychometric testing books and CDs.

www.How2Become.com

Attend a 1-day police recruitment course:
www.PoliceCourse.co.uk